UNEARTHED

a poetry collection by
Jaymie Joleen Schroeder

A publication of

Eber & Wein Publishing
Pennsylvania

Unearthed

Copyright © 2024 by Jaymie Joleen Schroeder
PC: TammyLynnPhotos.com

Library of Congress
Cataloging in Publication Data

ISBN 978-1-60880-765-9

Proudly manufactured in the United States of America by

Eber & Wein Publishing

Pennsylvania

Dedication

This poetry collection is dedicated to my family, particularly my heroes of the family. This book is dedicated to my two feet that finally mustered enough courage to flee from my domestic abuser. This book is dedicated to my heart that's continued strongly beating and opening itself up after countless years of emotional, physical, and sexual abuse from more avenues than I'd like to admit. This book is dedicated to my therapists: my certified therapist, the vivacious blondes at work that I've always looked up to and sought guidance from, and my batty friends I have who remain screaming in my corner with the largest of banners. I could not be more thankful for all of you.

This book is dedicated to you, all of you here blossoming with me through the pages that you're reading right now. I hope that any of those suffering now, before, or after us can find solace in some of this print. You are not alone.

My brother, thank you for: being my closest friend, loving me unconditionally, and being my biggest inspiration.

My teachers, all teachers, thank you for guiding the children that fight for a chance in this world each & every day.

For all of those here, this is my truth…
May you find *power* in it.

Contents

Paradisaeidae

You were,
A paradise bird.

I was rotting fruit that the
Flies picked at.

You swallowed me.
You consumed me.

You shit me back out.

You devour, everything.
You shit all over, anything.
When you spread your wings
You. Are. Ugly.

When one sees the carbon-black paradise bird
In the forest dancing for courtship,
His neon eyes and mouth
Searching to eat your soul…

It's already too late for you.

Strong Women

Strong women remember their roots
Acknowledge their scars
And choose for the pursuit of happiness
While supporting other women to do the same.

Snowflakes Can Fall In The Wrong Places

I would've waited forever to taste him
On the tip of my tongue
Because out of all the snowflakes in the sky
I thought that he was the only one for me.

Deathly Cold

I found comfort in his arms
When I was alone in the woods,
Because even the bones of an ash tree
Are sanctuary when you're desperately cold.

When Men Treat Women Like Packages

He takes pride in picking her out
Just the way that he likes her.
So much so
He's convinced her she's finally found
"Home."

She shows up magnificently dressed
And exceeding all expectations,
But even though he relays this information to her,
He receives her
And he opens her
When he wants to.

He knew that her main purpose in life
Was to please him,
That's why he chose her.
Yet, he ordered her to his home
Knowing that she won't.

He is selfish.

She should be cherished
And begs to be so,
In any form
Every single time that she
Or, a new package comes to the door again.

When men treat women like packages,
They should think of how fortunate they are
For each package that doesn't burn the house down.

When Men Are Her Major Flaw

If you haven't had sex on a roof
In a public park
Or on a kitchen table
Have you truly lived?

If you haven't nuzzled your nose into the side of his warm neck
Saturated the crow's feet on the corners of his eyes with
Your pursed lips
Or found safety buried in his chest as you
Traced the curves of his triceps
With your fingertips
Have you ever really found deep love?

If you haven't cried until your eyes burned hot
Talked down to the reflection of your red swollen face in the mirror
Or thrown your body to the floor so that you could bang
Your fists into the ground and scream
Have you truly suffered?

If you haven't only found peace in your heart
Through the body of a man
Cursed at God for deep-rooted childhood
Abandonment and neglect
Or wished yourself dead because your makers, and the man
Have always left you.
Consider yourself lucky
Because you may have never actually lost yourself.

I promise that there's only one way to grow, and that is to
Have sex with yourself
Learn to love yourself
And have mercy on yourself.

Are you finally ready to learn from your flaws?

4

I've Done Things

I've done things I wouldn't like to admit.
I've watched amphibians suffer
Because I wasn't brave, or kind
Enough to tell the boys in the sand
To stop blowing them up.

I've done things I wouldn't like to admit.
I've been crammed into small spaces
And forced to do ungodly things
Because I didn't know what else to do
Or how to get out.

I've done things I wouldn't like to admit.
As a young girl I prayed for my father
To save me from my life
Even if it meant he were to treat me like
The others,
Because I didn't care how any man treated me
If it meant that I would never be alone again.

I've done things I wouldn't like to admit.
I've had sex with strangers
And I've risked my own reputation
For men who don't care about me
Or men who tell me they're no longer
Intimate with their spouses.

I've done things I wouldn't like to admit.
I've done things.

We Are Like Wallpaper

Layers of our life can be peeled back
Like wallpaper.

You start out new
Pretty,
Untarnished.

Eventually, you begin to coat yourself
With new layers.

You become skeptical
Critical.
At times,
Ugly.

Before you know it
You'll pray to have the chance
To rip the layers off of your own back
In order to start fresh again.

Organic Love

Organic love is large
Like the ocean.

With organic love,
You share your deepest secrets
And your biggest aspirations
With each other.

Organic love
Never stops growing.
Whether the sun is shining or the sky is crying
You learn & grow, together.

In organic love,
Sometimes you hold hands in public
Sometimes you hold hands falling asleep.

Organic love is imperfect, but it
Never fails, never fails, never fails.

Volcano Girl

They say that red hair comes from
Sugar and fire.

I'm the sweetest birdsong on the mountainside
Ninety-five percent of the time, but
The remaining five percent of my time is spent
^^*^*^*^*^*^*^*^*^ dancing *^*^*^*^*^*^*^*^*^*^*
BeTweeN VariOUs StaGEs Of VoLCanIC ERUPTION

I've worn my volcano hair for over thirty years
And I've just now learned that you
Never should've expected
Anything less.

Thirteen

2004 School Year

I live to die
I'm dead inside
I'm tired of tasting
These tears that I cry.

One Cold Table

There are no guests at this
Old tattered wooden table
The gauges in the wood have seen
Little people dragged across the floor.

There have been one hundred times
That splinters on
The filthy legs that the children played around
Wished that they would never hear
The children's screams again.

When the table was finally passed down
There was relief in something warm finally being served for supper.
But, the table could still smell the absence of love in the air.

Trampled little children grew to be
Trampled little adults.
The air remained nauseating, and each room cold
Until the little adults learned that they could find a new table.

Journeying

An effervescent sun gleams
On the warm tips of each
Towering cornstalk reflecting off of her copper shades,
And every time the black shepherd looks up at her with his
Hazel chestnut eyes she wonders,
"What's ahead on this journey?"

A 90s hit blares like the wind rushing through her auburn hair as she
reminisces about
"What's been loved?"
"What's been lost?"
And every day her first question,
"Why haven't I been that someone special?!"

The vibrations around her
Spinning wheels create colors that twirl along the open road
And disappear
Into a distant memory
Like the Cuervo that he was once so devoted to, or,
Like dirt in the air.
Now the only remnant of
That love
Is an invisible bottle
And a slice of life
That only him & her will ever even know
Truly existed.

She dances to her own rhythm of
Beats bumping on the open road through her pearly white four-door
anyways,
And she realizes that the beats are dancing to their own rhythm on
the road too!

He can pretend that it wasn't real
Or that he'll forget,
But, he knows,
And, she knows...
"That's a Lie," a Maury voice shrieks!

The dust clouds trail her treads on the
Old familiar rocky road where she
Struggles with somber sober symphonies
That fill the back of her Mazda,
& "No!" She won't ever really want to actually
Talk about "It!"
How can she be "Top notch,"
And not anybody's "Prime pick?!"

She is that rose
That he chose
Then pulled out of
Again & again.
Eventually, he tossed her
Into the trash bin
With the dried-out corn husks

And she lost herself in the blinding sunrise as her
Tawny hair & the amber shreds
Blended together in the heat of
The driver's side window.
Yet, she journeyed on,
She remembered,
And she stood strong!

Submersible

You are the fire that burns in a heart
Which was once colder than
Bones on the floor in the bathroom.

Everywhere, I searched for God.
Everyone, let me drown in the water.

I walked. I prayed. I found you.
And you pulled me out.

Love & Heroin

Loving him,
Is like loving Heroin.

The needle in your arm hurts
But, the poking sensation is quickly replaced
With false fuzzy feelings of: warmth, safety, euphoria.
You feel better than you've ever felt in your life,
You'll risk anything and everything
For him.
You choose him over everything.
He hurts you,
He drains you,
He makes you sick.
You run back to him for the fuzzy feelings,
But he takes everything away from you.
You continue choosing him over everything,
You lose everything.
You're hanging onto your life by a thread for the false feelings
That mean
Nothing.
He will take and take and take until you've got nothing left,
He will kill you if you don't stop loving him.

Loving Him,
Is like loving Heroin.

To The Woman He Brought To Our Protection Hearing

I bet that even though you
Thought that you knew me
You never thought for a second
That I was once you.

Well, let me tell you
Right this second
And, the second after that
And, the second that I stood there stabbing the floor
With my high heels...

Like he stabbed me in my face with his lies
Like you both stabbed me through my heart with
Your double entendres,
"You are me two years ago."

I Wonder Now

It's been 880 days, 22 hours, 36 minutes and 23 seconds since I left
That hotel room.

I wonder now
If we were doomed from the start, or if we're meant for
Something bigger.

I wonder now
If we told ourselves lies all along, or if we just told each other lies.

I wonder now
If we'll survive together
Die together, or die with
Broken hearts.

I wonder now
If either one of us are capable of being loved
Or, if we just never deserved love in the first place.

I wonder now
How many people we've truly lost since we've met,
Including ourselves.

I wonder now
If we will ever find salvation.

I wonder now.

Even The Beautiful Make You Bleed

Like still water on a desolate mountain
He takes hold of me.

I am captivated as I take in each of his breaths
Because, for one of the very first times in my life
I feel escape.

I feel safe with him.
For, usually, the rage of a country burns in my mind.

In my moments with him the seismic shakes of the world are stilled.
Even the alligators and the mosquitos cannot threaten that.

When You Told Me

When you told me
Your New Girl
Was way finer than me
Did you think about the moments
You told me
I was the most beautiful woman
You had ever seen?

Did you realize
When you told me
Your New Girl
Was a woman from your "past," it was after
You told me
There was no New Girl
Because you loved me so deeply
You couldn't even dream of being with someone else?

When you told me
Your New Girl
Would pick out your new shower curtain so I could
Keep the one still hanging next to your smirk
Did you remember telling me that you would never
Let anyone ever hurt me again?

When you told
Your New Girl
That you wanted to marry her that summer
Did you reminisce about telling me
The very same thing earlier that spring?

Did you think about the moments
That you would have to face a monster in the mirror
When you told me?

Dig

I remember when "Dig"
Was an Incubus song
That you said made you think of me
While you held my hand
Whispered into my ear
And stared into my soul.

Dig is now outreach
I grapple for
While I suffocate in silence...

      Drowning in water

          Burning in fire, and

              Bleeding in love.

When You Know You've Met Agony

You know you've met agony
When you look in the mirror
To ask yourself to stop begging God
To let you see at least one moment
On this planet

Where you can say
"I've beat him,"

Because he's no longer good trouble
& he can no longer beat you.

Continued Seasons

He may give you Easter flowers
Pretend to like your daughters,
And hide his guns from you...
But, stop smiling at me.

This is only your beginning,
For he is continuing the seasons with you.

Flowers get replaced with
Blunt trauma to your face that stitches can't fix.

He refuses to like any daughters–especially his own,
And the sound of a gun cocking will
One day be a way you typically
Awake from your sleep.

He asked me to marry him this past spring,
Before he applied for your marriage certificate
With you this past summer.
Before he was with you feeding off of deep regret
He was buying my mother and I flowers.

The Sex Machine

His ice cubes left his luscious lips
Colder than his sweet lies did.
He slid the ice cube down the side of my neck before it
Grazed my shoulder
And moved across my breasts.
Even as he drew lines with the ice cube
Up and down my shattered chest
His body, mind, and soul felt colder.
If I could go back in time
I would've never traded my body, mind, and soul for his ice cubes.

You Killed My Heart

What brought on
Rivers of blood
On my arms
Was less painful
Than the thoughts about
All of the moments
That I can now find six foot holes in.
I refused to see the flies,
Because I loved you.

The Fighter

My heart, and my mind
Have my body constantly chained to a
Ball at the bottom of water so murky that I am invisible.

The moments that I can find opportunity to hit the surface
For a breath of air
Or the strength to fight for a breath,
Those are the only moments that I have
Freedom in my heart, and in my mind.

What's got me in chains will never go away
But, what's still got me fighting for breaths
Will never go away either.

To Thou Who Shall Not Be Named

When you were sixteen I was brought into this world.
When you were forty-eight you tried to
Drive knives through my heart,
And bury my body beneath
The lead dirt in the backyard.

But, little did we know I am stronger than you.

The ghosts of your past, & mine
Helped me carry my bones to the rooftop.
From there we watched you
Bury yourself beneath the floorboards.

We will eternally carry ourselves above you
With innocence, grace, & pride
For never having committed any of your crimes.

My Only Crime

Falling for you was a sin
That I will carry to the grave.

Instead of running from the
Burning building,
I ran into you.

I wonder if every time that someone looks at me
They see the scars on my face?
Scars that hold not only my pain,
But theirs.

For, I ran into that
Burning building
For you.

Only to leave
Everyone else
To starve in the street.

God Saved Me From Becoming Nothing

His words were like

Waste baskets.

Sometimes, empty.

Sometimes, seemingly full.

Always destined for the landfill.

I cried until my

Eyes bled.

Now, I laugh

And I laugh.

Periods and Provocation

There are two kinds of periods.
Light, heavy, and miscarriage.

A child thinks she's dying if
She's never been taught what a period is.

A child doesn't argue if
She doesn't know what an abortion is.

A child doesn't know not to tell anyone
If she doesn't know that she's the only one excited to
Have a baby.

A child that doesn't get taught why she's fumed her parents
Probably won't learn to understand why
She's fumed the man who wants an abortion
Or, what "producing" means in her world.

Blossoming into something that's not
Sickeningly sweet
Takes learning about
More than flowers, periods, and provocation.

Savor These Moments

My eyes find the light reflecting off of his
Long jet black eyelashes
While the curtains dance together through the open window.

I admire his handsome face as the morning breeze rolls toward us,
And he sleeps ever so peacefully.
I find my own peace in the calmness
Of his breaths.

I search for constellations in the freckles
On his gorgeously high cheekbones
Until the dog forces me up
With his soggy-eyes, bright spirit, and stuffed animal
That we call "Fox."

I realize that I live for these moments.

Dead Apologies

Undoubtedly, I can live without your apologies.
But, I yearn for them.

In consideration of all of my trauma from you
And your four wives before me
You owe us that much.

"I'm sorry."
"I'm evil."
"I'm screwed up."
Wouldn't that bring all of us peace?

But, you will
Never apologize.

In order to make certain that
Women no longer scream at your
Hands wrapped around their throats
In their own kitchens
On their own back porches
And at the infrequent public occasions
Where you will always follow "your girl" to the bathroom
All that we can do...

Is acknowledge the ones before and after us
Stand tall with anyone that is brave enough,
And hold hands with those that have survived you.

Holidays, subways, or courthouses might be
Off of limits for you
But, in these public spaces
We can fight back, together.

Undoubtedly, I can live without your apologies.

I Promise

You can get over it
Even though you thought that you never would.

Comfort Can Be A Cage

Love does not come without stepping outside of
Your comfort zone, failing, and growing.

Love does not exist without pain,
Ever.

We live.
We love.
We die.

Without love,
We do not truly live.

Without stepping outside of our cages of comfort,
We do not find opportunities to love.

Without risks,
We will leave this world empty.

Step outside of your cage,
Fall on your face.
Try again.
Comfort can be a cage.

Valentine's Day

If you don't buy her flowers,
You're a fucking asshole.
If you don't tell her she's beautiful,
Someone else will.
If you're not faithful to her,
Someone else can be.

If you're incapable of loving her the way that you should.
Let. Her. Go.

Soulmates

A soulmate will drop their heart out into
Your ocean, on purpose,
So that you can carry it forever.

Maybe never deserted
Maybe once deserted
Maybe always deserted
This heart's now dropped for
You.

Burning, bloody, or cold,
At your worst and at your best,
A soulmate inspires
You.

Once you find your soulmate
You'll know that they've always believed in
And been destined for
You.

The Man With The Devil Tattoos

His devilish web will reel you in
Long before you see his life of sin
He is manipulative, calculating, and far from stupid
He surrounds himself with only those he finds suited.

He'll promise you the world while he boasts of himself with a toast
While he stays quietly concerned about those who might see he's
A ghost.
In a singular moment he knows if someone is a risk to his cover
Thus he hides himself and you from all of those who might discover.

He sees himself in the devil plastered on his back and his shaved
Head
He will pray on the innocent until the day that he's dead.
He's full of fire and in time he constantly implodes
Eventually a day will come where you know that he will always
Reload.

By the time you've finally decided you know you have to run
The real dangers to you will only have just begun.
Keep in mind that domestic hotlines do exist
And please utilize them in situations like this.

Remind yourself of all the times that he's held your face to the earth
And isolated you from those that you have known since birth.
He will never be worth it so please let him go
For his devilish spirit is all that will ever grow.

There Is No Shame In Deep Love

He took my trust
He took my devotion
He took my loyalty
He took a lot of my hope,
He even took my most valuable belongings.

But, he did not take my dignity
He did not take my respect
He did not take my intelligence
He did not take my compassion,
And he most certainly did not take my self-worth.

I am better today.
I am better tomorrow.
I am better here on out.

Be Kind to Your Sisters

Never be mean to your sisters,
But know we've all done it.

Sisters wine
Sisters cry
Sisters fight
And sisters die…

Be kind to your sisters.

The World's Oldest Profession

I promise you,
That no woman in the history of forever
Has ever wanted to sell her body.

The world has always been fucked up.

I tell you,
Here and now
That women have always had to make "choices."

I assure you,
That a woman would never want to give away her
Spirit to a man in acclamation of marriage
Like a woman would never want to give away her body
In restitution of justness.

With words of honor I can say…
That if women were not caged
If women were not forced to be doubted
And, If women were not abused
Women would never sell their bodies.

Pain

Can
Become
Power.

About the Author

Jaymie Joleen Schroeder is a University of Nebraska at Omaha Chancellor's award-winning graduate from the College of Education. Her endorsements are K-12 Art education and English 7-12 education.

A couple of years prior to the pandemic, Jaymie left the field of education due to personal health conflicts. When she turned in her teaching badge at the largest district in the state of Nebraska, she was teaching over 1800 students at two separate schools on opposite ends of Omaha. Although the district and her students begged her to stay, Jaymie knew she had to leave the field of education if she was ever to become a mentally and/or physically healthy person for herself.

Fortunately, Jaymie was welcomed and eager to go back to her previous job at her family's roofing company—the best roofing company in their region. Shortly after resigning from education, Jaymie became motivated in hiring her education in the field of construction, and she received a promotion at her family's construction company. Jaymie was also diagnosed with severe Post-traumatic stress disorder at this time (PTSD). This diagnosis explained life-long challenges that internally affected her.

Childhood years helped to cultivate the very best aspects of Jaymie's persona but also some of the most harmful. Her complex PTSD stems from childhood, adolescent, and adult trauma. Bipolar, depression, severe anxiety disorder, alcohol use disorder, panic disorder, social anxiety disorder, and borderline personality disorder are diagnoses that have also affected Jaymie throughout her life.

Jaymie spent much of her childhood years with her grandmother where she learned to "practice kind." "From my grandmother I learned manners, respect, gratitude, and what routines looked like. I will forever be thankful for the days she spent holding me accountable to make my bed by 7 AM—without her I wouldn't have had a chance in this world."

During her adolescent years, Jaymie struggled to focus, fit in, or value herself. "I spent the majority of my adolescent years hunched over staring at the ground beneath my feet. I felt stupid, I felt ugly, and I felt unworthy of being loved. I dropped out of high school at the age of eighteen, having passed a singular Art course and a singular English course. I was also pregnant from an inappropriate relationship that had already been going on for five years. As a ward of the state, I had one caseworker who believed in me . . . He encouraged me to give college a shot and made me realize it was an option for me. After proving to myself that I could successfully complete college courses, the sky was the limit for me. Despite dropping out of high school, I had successfully worked my way up to landing a teaching position at Omaha's largest school district before I even walked across the University of Nebraska at Omaha graduation stage. For once in my life, I had some choices."

Today, Jaymie is the National Women in Roofing Nebraska Chapter Secretary. She is a nationally published poet, professional model, domestic abuse advocate/survivor, anorexia/bulimia advocate/survivor, and sober living advocate/survivor. Jaymie is proud to be passionate about the arts, women empowerment, construction, human relations, cultural awareness, and animals. Painting, modeling, and above all writing are creative outlets for Jaymie. Writing is her therapy. Writing is how she copes and heals. Writing is how she can find the most meaningful words to speak.

It is Jaymie's hope that this writing inspires you to find or continue with your own creative and/or therapeutic endeavors.

Resources

Aacap. "Trauma and Child Abuse Resource Center." *Child Abuse Resource Center*. https://www.aacap.org/aacap/Families_and_ Youth/Resource_Centers/Child_Abuse_Resource_Center/Home. aspx.

American Pregnancy Association. 30 Sept. 2022. https://american pregnancy.org.

"Home." *Lifeline*. https://988lifeline.org.

"National Domestic Violence Hotline." *The Hotline*. 13 June 2022. https://www.thehotline.org.

"National Hotlines." *Victim Connect Resource Center*. 16 Feb. 2021. https://victimconnect.org/resources/national-hotlines.

National Human Trafficking Hotline. https://humantraffickinghotline. org.

"National Organization for Women." *National Organization for Women*. 2 Dec. 2022. https://now.org.

"National Sexual Assault Hotline: Confidential 24/7 Support." *RAINN*. https://www.rainn.org/resources.

"Resource Centers." *The Administration for Children and Families*. https://www.acf.hhs.gov/fysb/fv-centers.

"Suicide Prevention." *National Institute of Mental Health*. US De partment of Health and Human Services. https://www.nimh.nih. gov/health/topics/suicide-prevention.

"Samhsa's National Helpline: Samhsa-Substance Abuse and Mental Health Services Administration." *SAMHSA*. https://www.sam hsa.gov/find-help/national-helpline.